LEARN Cursive
WITH
DRAWING

OVER 100 PAGES OF WRITING AND DRAWING ACTIVITIES
TO LEARN AND IMPROVE HANDWRITING

Seaside Study

Copyright © 2024 Seaside Study

All rights reserved. No part of this book may be reproduced, photocopied, or used in any manner without the prior written permission of the copyright owner, except for brief quotations in a book review.

FREE DIGITAL HANDWRITING PAGES.

Thank you for choosing our book! Visit Seasidestudy.com to download more handwriting pages and continue your handwriting journey.

free book

We want to see your work! Share your fantastic finished handwriting pages with us.

 @seaside.study

Scan me for more pages.

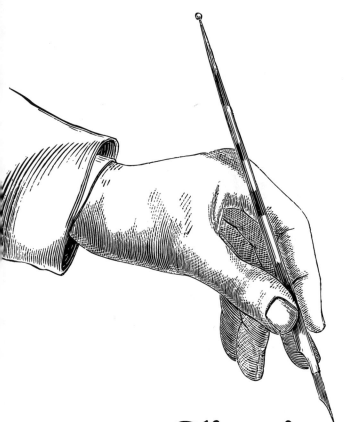

This book belongs to:

_____

TABLE OF CONTENTS

1   10 Tips to Improve Handwriting
    Learn ten effective strategies to improve handwriting proficiency, regardless of skill level, and enhance clarity and fluidity in writing.

4   Chapter 1: Letters
    In this chapter, we focus on mastering the fundamentals of letter writing through step-by-step lessons, refining your penmanship, stroke by stroke.

34 Chapter 2: Drawing and Writing
    In this chapter, we merge the worlds of drawing and handwriting, offering step-by-step drawing lessons paired with tailored writing prompts to fuel your creativity.

92 Chapter 3: Free Writing
    Welcome to a chapter where creativity flourishes freely. Dive into boundless expression as you draw, write, and explore, whether crafting original creations or refining your skills in both handwriting and drawing.

10 TIPS TO IMPROVE HANDWRITING

1. Posture Matters

Sit up straight with both feet flat on the ground. Good posture supports proper alignment of your hand and wrist, making it easier to control your movements.

2. Relax Your Grip

Hold your pen or pencil gently, with your fingers forming a tripod grip (thumb and two fingers). Avoid gripping too tightly, which can lead to fatigue and cramped fingers.

3. Consistency is Key

Strive for consistent letter size and spacing. This uniformity makes your handwriting more legible and aesthetically pleasing.

4. Sloped Writing

Angle your paper slightly to the left if you're right-handed and to the right if you're left-handed. This allows your hand to move more freely and reduces smudging.

5. Practice Letter Formation

Pay attention to how each letter is formed. Consistent and correct letter formation is vital for legibility. Utilize lined paper to help with letter height and spacing.

6. Slow Down

Take your time when writing. Rushing can lead to sloppy handwriting. As you practice, you'll naturally become faster without sacrificing quality.

7. Use the Right Tools

Choose a pen or pencil that feels comfortable in your hand. Experiment with different writing instruments until you find the one that best suits you.

8. Warm-Up Exercises

Before writing, do a few warm-up exercises to loosen your hand and wrist. Simple doodles and loops on your paper can help prepare your muscles for writing.

9. Patience and Perseverance

Remember that improving your handwriting takes time. Be patient with yourself, and don't get discouraged by initial challenges.

10. Seek Feedback

Ask friends, family, or teachers to review your handwriting and offer constructive feedback. Sometimes, an outside perspective can help identify areas for improvement.

Chapter 1

Letters

Welcome to a chapter dedicated to mastering the art of letter writing. Here, we embark on a journey to refine your penmanship, step by step. Through carefully crafted lessons, we'll guide you in practicing each letter, ensuring precision and elegance in every stroke. Get ready to elevate your handwriting skills as we delve into the fundamentals, laying the foundation for beautiful and expressive lettering.

Cursive Alphabet

A B C D E F G
H I J K L M
N O P Q R S T
U V W X Y Z

a b c d e f g h i
j k l m n o p q r
s t u v w x y z

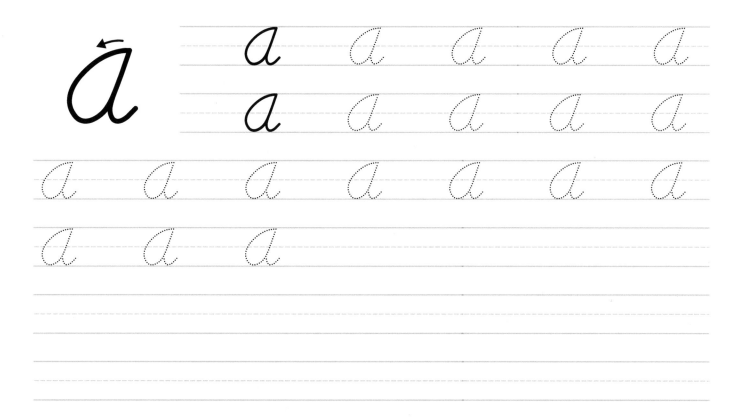

astronaut

a b c d e f g h i j k l m n o p q r s t u v w x y z

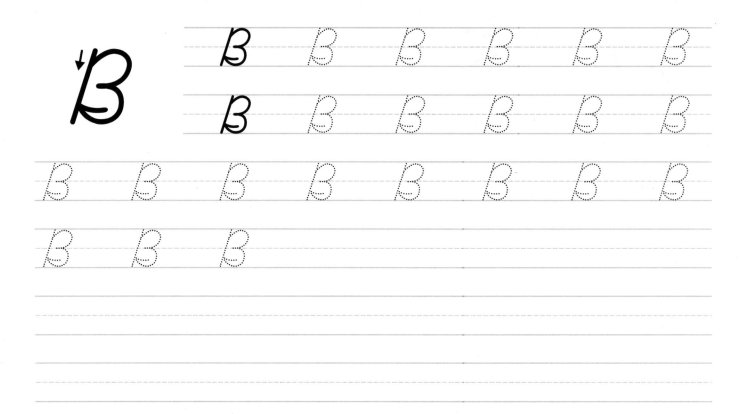

butterfly

a b **c** d e f g h i j k l m n o p q r s t u v w x y z

cat

a b c **d** e f g h i j k l m n o p q r s t u v w x y z

dog

a b c d **e** f g h i j k l m n o p q r s t u v w x y z

E E E E E E E
E E E E E E E
E E E E E E E
E E E

e e e e e e
e e e e e e e
e e e e e e e
e e e

eye

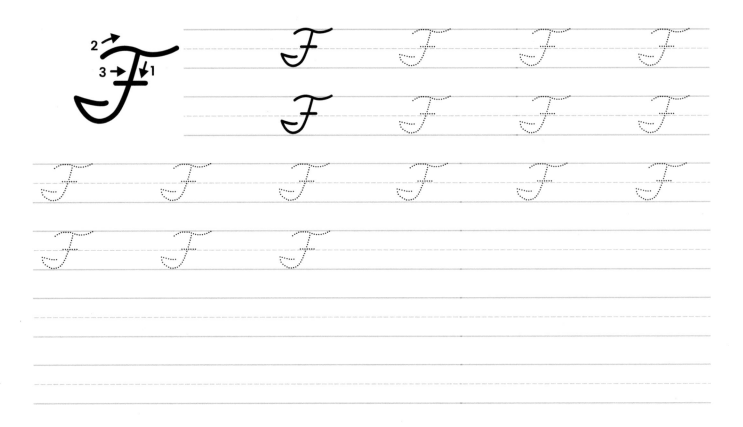

flower

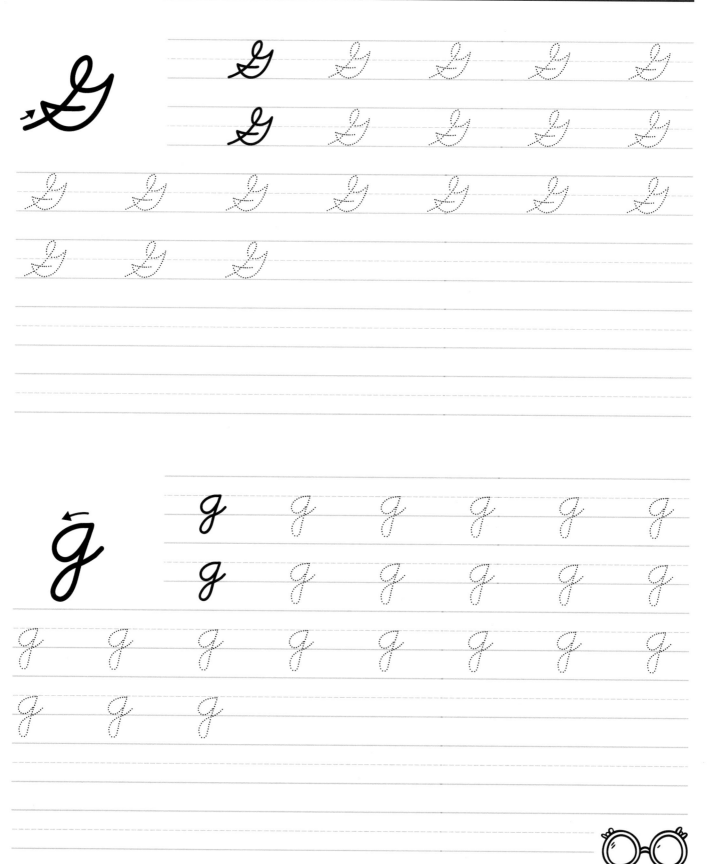

glasses

heart

a b c d e f g h **i** j k l m n o p q r s t u v w x y z

ice cream

a b c d e f g h i **j** k l m n o p q r s t u v w x y z

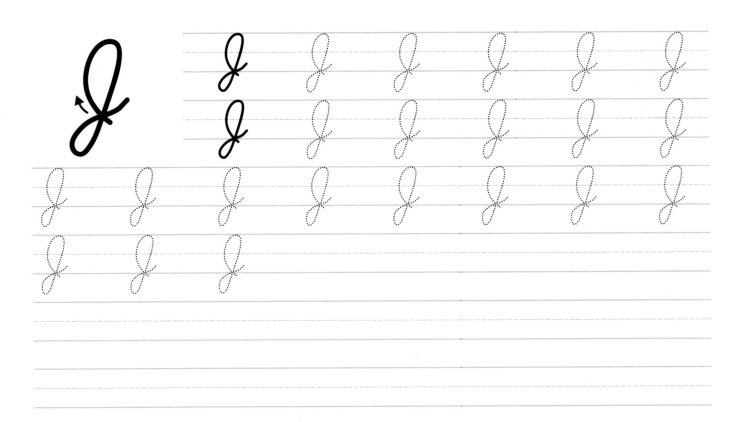

jam

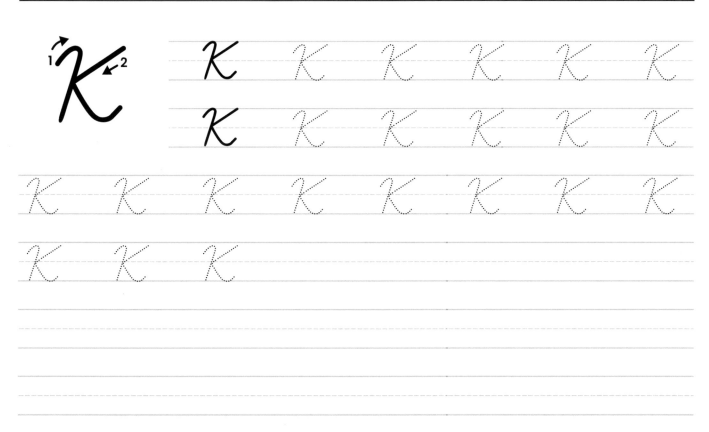

kite

16

light

a b c d e f g h i j k l **m** n o p q r s t u v w x y z

m

moon

a b c d e f g h i j k l m **n** o p q r s t u v w x y z

a b c d e f g h i j k l m n **o** p q r s t u v w x y z

O

o

owl

| a | b | c | d | e | f | g | h | i | j | k | l | m | n | o | **p** | q | r | s | t | u | v | w | x | y | z |

paper airplane

a b c d e f g h i j k l m n o p **q** r s t u v w x y z

2

2 2 2 2 2 2
2 2 2 2 2 2
2 2 2 2 2 2 2
2 2 2

q

q q q q q q
q q q q q q
q q q q q q q
q q q

quilt

a b c d e f g h i j k l m n o p q **r** s t u v w x y z

radio

a b c d e f g h i j k l m n o p q r **s** t u v w x y z

stars

a b c d e f g h i j k l m n o p q r s **t** u v w x y z

turtle

| a | b | c | d | e | f | g | h | i | j | k | l | m | n | o | p | q | r | s | t | **u** | v | w | x | y | z |

𝓤

𝓾

umbrella

a b c d e f g h i j k l m n o p q r s t u **v** w x y z

vase

a b c d e f g h i j k l m n o p q r s t u v **w** x y z

W

w

wand

a b c d e f g h i j k l m n o p q r s t u v w x y z

x-ray

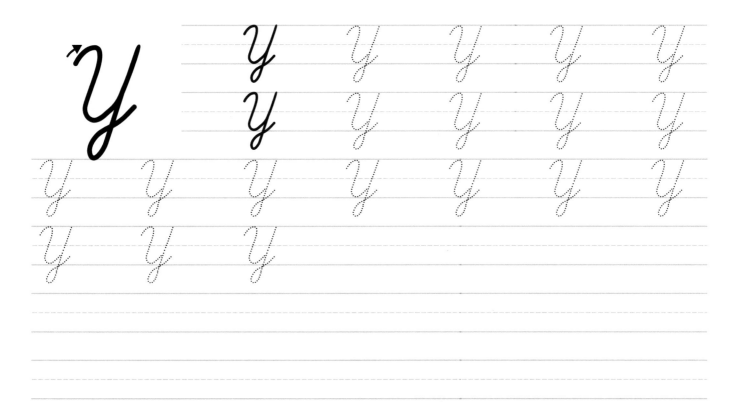

a b c d e f g h i j k l m n o p q r s t u v w x y z

zebra

Chapter 2

Drawing and Writing

Welcome to the chapter where we seamlessly blend the beauty of drawing with the elegance of handwriting. Here, we embark on a journey that intertwines the strokes of your pen with the lines of your sketches. We'll guide you through step-by-step drawing lessons, and with each picture you bring to life, we'll inspire you with writing prompts tailored to ignite your imagination. Get ready to let your creativity flow as we merge the realms of drawing and writing, transforming blank pages into vibrant canvases of expression in an interactive and engaging way.

STEP-BY-STEP TUTORIAL

how to draw a
fox

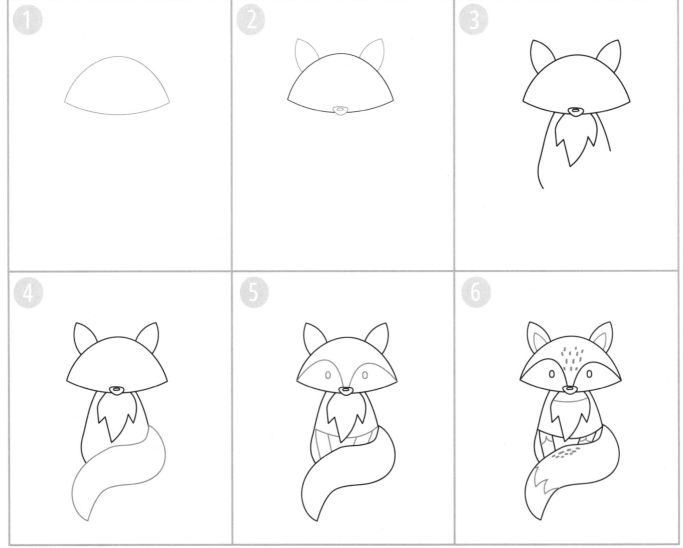

Draw a fox.

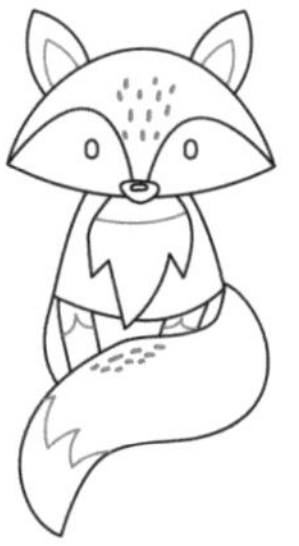

Trace and write the word.

fox fox

fox fox

Draw a fox.

Trace the sentence.

Foxes are clever with bushy tails and pointy ears.

Write the sentence.

Trace the sentence.

Foxes playfully chase each other through the grass.

Write the sentence.

Draw and write about foxes.

STEP-BY-STEP TUTORIAL

how to draw a *butterfly*

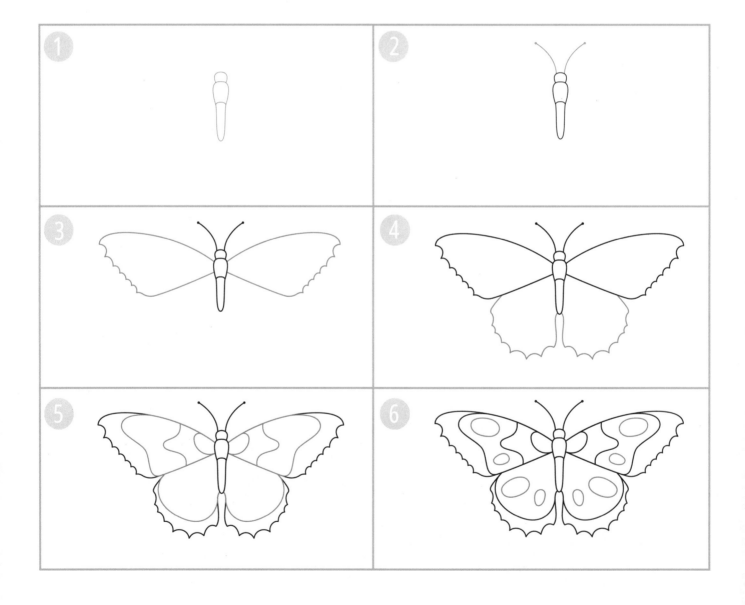

Draw a butterfly.

Trace and write the word.

butterfly *butterfly*

butterfly *butterfly*

Draw a butterfly.

Trace the sentence.

From caterpillars, they transform into butterflies.

Write the sentence.

Trace the sentence.

Some butterflies migrate thousands of miles each year.

Write the sentence.

Draw and write about butterflies.

STEP-BY-STEP TUTORIAL

how to draw a
flower

Draw a flower.

Trace and write the word.

flower　　　　　*flower*
flower　　　　　*flower*

Draw a flower.

Trace the sentence.

Flowers come in all shapes and sizes.

Write the sentence.

Trace the sentence.

Drawing a flower is creating a tiny garden on paper.

Write the sentence.

Draw and write about flowers.

STEP-BY-STEP TUTORIAL
how to draw a *lemon*

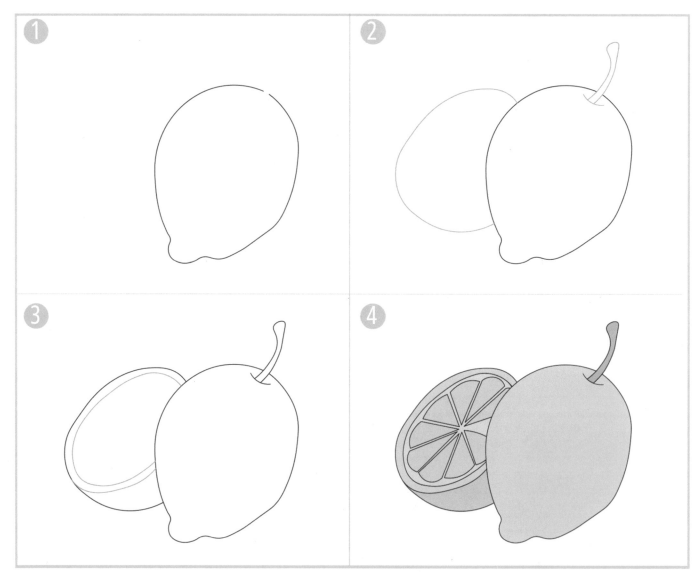

Draw a lemon.

Trace and write the word.

lemon   *lemon*
lemon   *lemon*

Draw a lemon.

Trace the sentence.

You can find lemon trees in warm, sunny places.

Write the sentence.

Trace the sentence.

Lemons are citrus fruits that grow on trees.

Write the sentence.

Draw and write about lemons.

STEP-BY-STEP TUTORIAL

how to draw a *airplane*

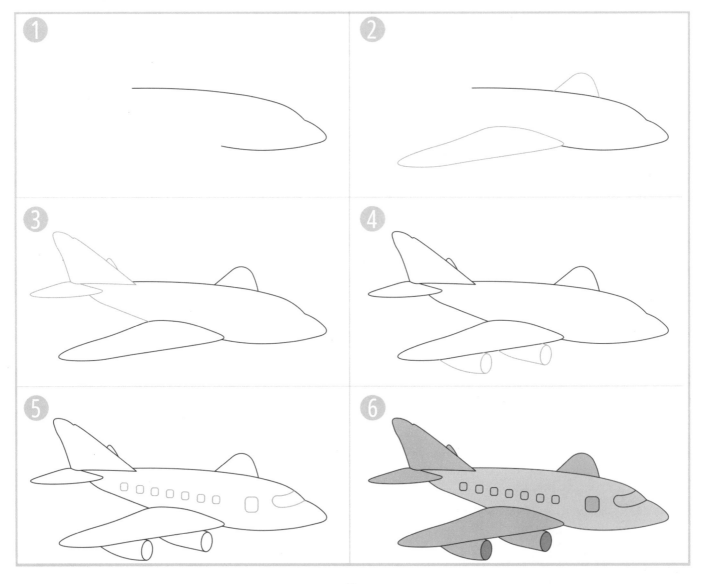

Draw an airplane.

Trace and write the word.

airplane   *airplane*
airplane   *airplane*

Draw an airplane.

Trace the sentence.

Airplanes have wings and a tail to help them soar.

Write the sentence.

Trace the sentence.

People travel long distances quickly by airplane.

Write the sentence.

Draw and write about airplanes.

STEP-BY-STEP TUTORIAL
how to draw a *turtle*

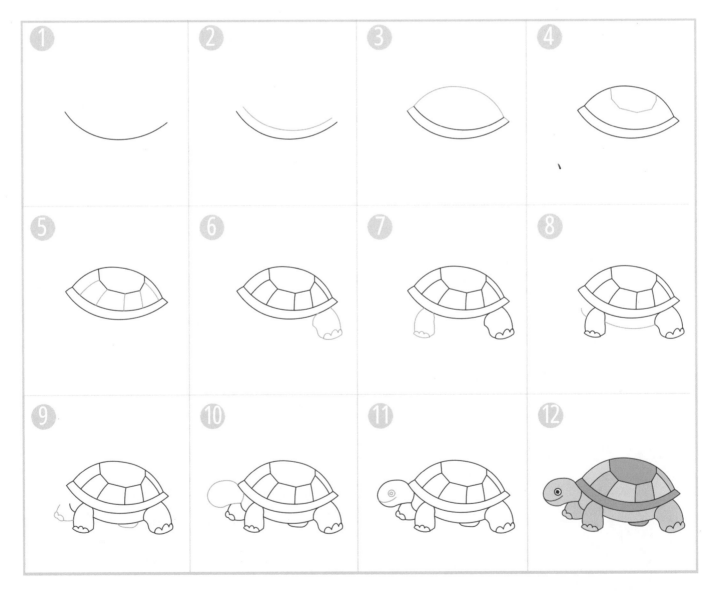

Draw a turtle.

Trace and write the word.

turtle   *turtle*

turtle   *turtle*

Draw a turtle.

Trace the sentence.

Some turtles can live both on land and in water.

Write the sentence.

Trace the sentence.

Turtles move slowly but can live a long time.

Write the sentence.

Draw and write about turtles.

STEP-BY-STEP TUTORIAL

how to draw a *fish*

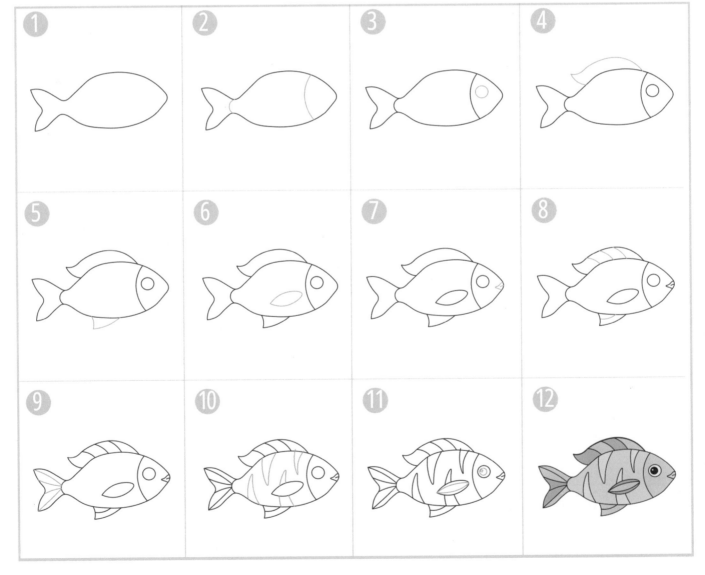

Draw a fish.

Trace and write the word.

fish
fish   *fish*
             fish

Draw a fish.

Trace the sentence.

Fish live in water and breathe through gills.

Write the sentence.

Trace the sentence.

Fish swim by moving their fins and tails.

Write the sentence.

Draw and write about fish.

STEP-BY-STEP TUTORIAL
how to draw a *giraffe*

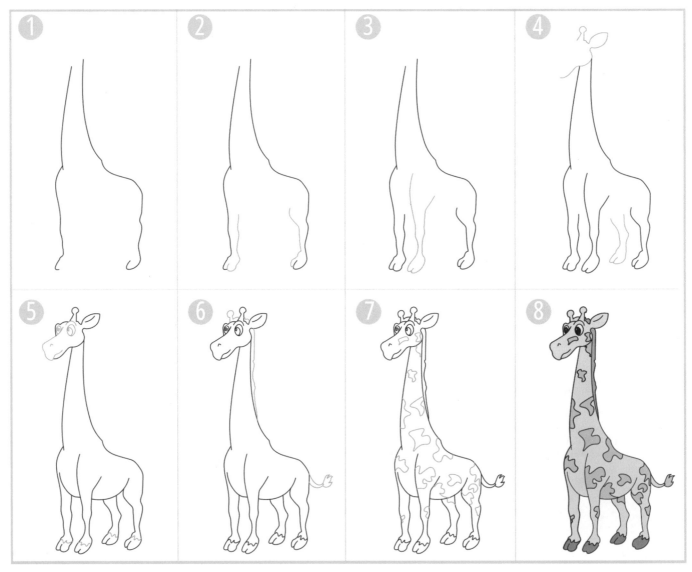

Draw a giraffe.

Trace and write the word.

giraffe

Draw a giraffe.

Trace the sentence.

Giraffes have long necks to reach leaves high in trees.

Write the sentence.

Trace the sentence.

Giraffes have unique spots for camouflage.

Write the sentence.

Draw and write about giraffes.

STEP-BY-STEP TUTORIAL
how to draw a
dog

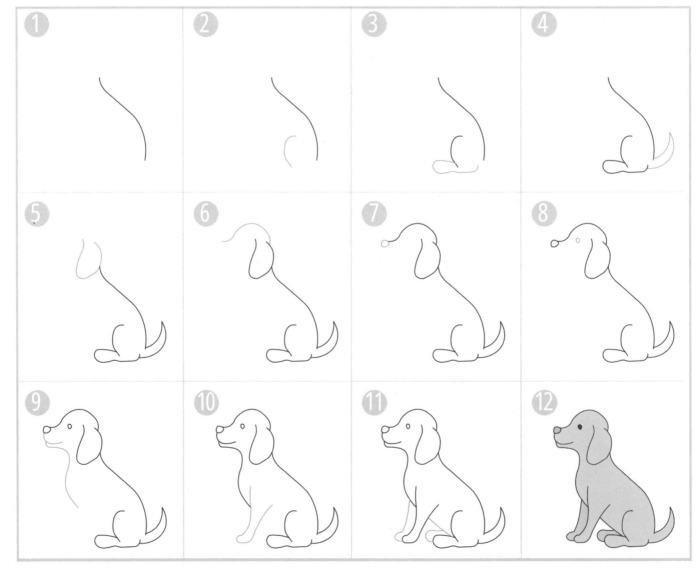

Draw a dog.

Trace and write the word.

dog

Draw a dog.

Trace the sentence.

Dogs have a keen sense of smell, hearing, and sight.

Write the sentence.

Trace the sentence.

The dogs love to play fetch with a ball.

Write the sentence.

Draw and write about dogs.

STEP-BY-STEP TUTORIAL
how to draw a *cat*

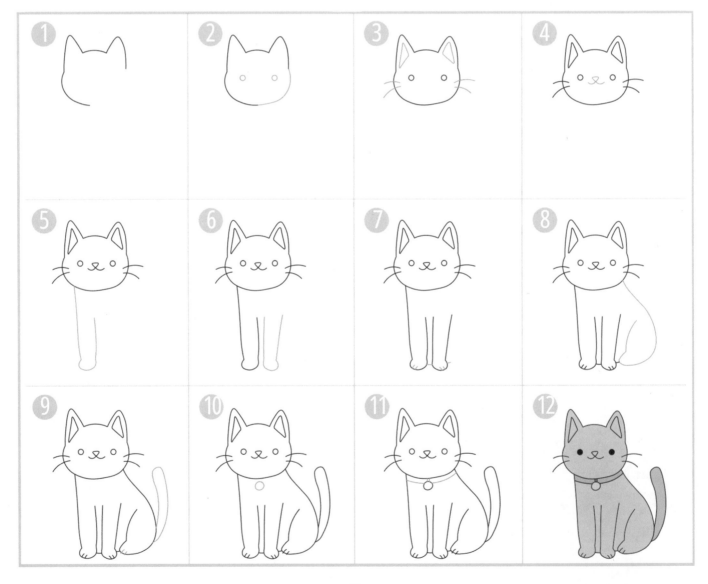

Draw a cat.

Trace and write the word.

cat   cat

cat   cat

Draw a cat.

Trace the sentence.

The cat plays with yarn, jumping and having fun.

Write the sentence.

Trace the sentence.

The cat naps in a cozy bed, dreaming of mice.

Write the sentence.

Draw and write about cats.

STEP-BY-STEP TUTORIAL
how to draw a *rabbit*

Draw a rabbit.

Trace and write the word.

rabbit   rabbit
rabbit   rabbit

Draw a rabbit.

Trace the sentence.

Rabbits have strong back legs that help them hop quickly.

Write the sentence.

Trace the sentence.

Rabbits are small furry animals with long ears.

Write the sentence.

Draw and write about rabbits.

STEP-BY-STEP TUTORIAL
how to draw a *boat*

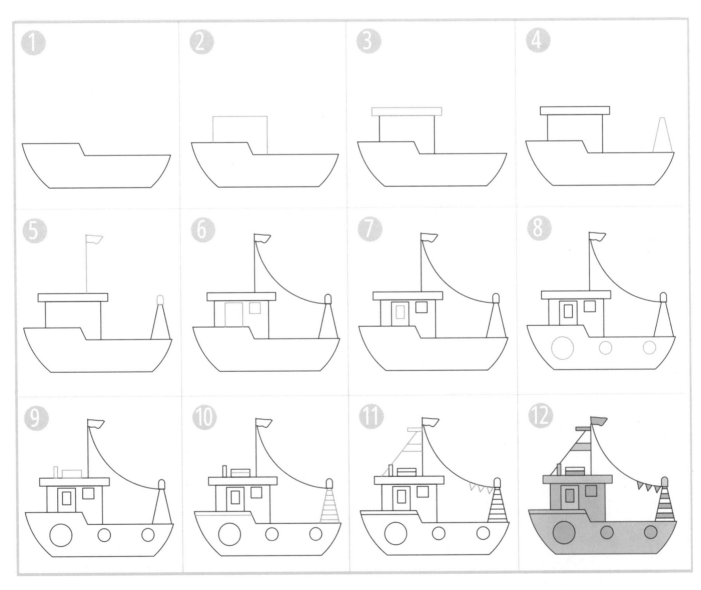

Draw a boat.

Trace and write the word.

boat   *boat*

boat   *boat*

Draw a boat.

Trace the sentence.

Boats are vehicles that travel on water.

Write the sentence.

Trace the sentence.

Boats are important for exploring oceans and rivers.

Write the sentence.

Draw and write about boats.

STEP-BY-STEP TUTORIAL
how to draw a
tree

Draw a tree.

Trace and write the word.

tree   *tree*

tree   *tree*

Draw a tree.

Trace the sentence.

Trees have green leaves that rustle in the wind.

Write the sentence.

Trace the sentence.

Trees give us fresh air and provide shade on sunny days.

Write the sentence.

Draw and write about trees.

STEP-BY-STEP TUTORIAL

how to draw a *crocodile*

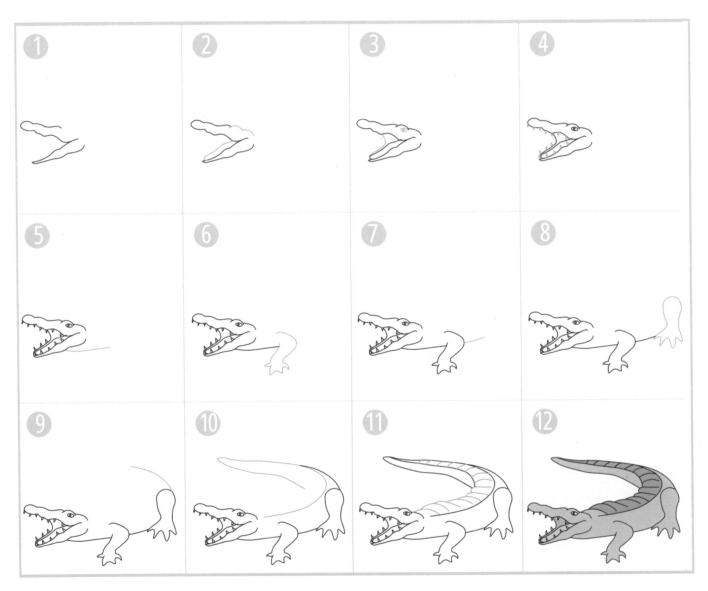

Draw a crocodile.

Trace and write the word.

crocodile crocodile

crocodile crocodile

Draw a crocodile.

Trace the sentence.

The big crocodile basks in the warm sun.

Write the sentence.

Trace the sentence.

Crocodile splashes in the river, doing a wiggle dance.

Write the sentence.

Draw and write about crocodiles.

७

Chapter 3

Free Writing

Welcome to a free chapter where creativity knows no bounds. We invite you to unleash your imagination through free writing and drawing. With ample space to let your ideas flow, whether crafting your creations or simply honing your cursive and drawing skills, this chapter is your canvas for expression and exploration.

Please
Leave a review

Thank you for choosing the Cursive with Drawing book. We are a family-owned business that initially started by creating books for our children. We enjoyed the process so much that we decided to create books for more kids like yours. Your honest review of our book would be highly appreciated as it helps us to spread the word about our hard work. We value your feedback, and it will help others decide whether this book suits them. Writing an Amazon review is an easy and quick way to help a small business and pass cursive handwriting skills to future generations.

Thank You!

Seaside Study

Scan this QR code using a smartphone to be directed to Amazon's review page for this book.

Made in the USA
Thornton, CO
05/27/25 23:39:12

332fa7bf-b8a8-44ba-9264-7faf17a2df8aR01